D1187737

Pebble® Plus

Understanding Differences

Some Kids Wear
Leg Braces

Revised Edition

Lola M Schaefer

raintree

a Capstone company — publishers for children

Raintree is an imprint of Capstone Global Library Limited,
a company incorporated in England and Wales having its
registered office at 264 Banbury Road, Oxford, OX2 7DY –
Registered company number: 6695582

www.raintree.co.uk
myorders@raintree.co.uk

Editorial credits
Sarah Bennett, designer; Tracy Cummins, media researcher;
Laura Manthe, production specialist

Photo credits
Capstone Studio: Karon Dubke, Cover, 5, 9, 11, 13, 15, 17, 21;
Getty Images: KidStock, 7; iStockphoto: duaneellison, 19

Printed and bound in India

ISBN 978 1 4747 5690 7
22 21 20 19 18
10 9 8 7 6 5 4 3 2 1

British Library Cataloguing in Publication Data
A full catalogue record for this book is available from the
British Library.

Contents

How leg braces help

Some kids wear leg braces.

Leg braces support
weak or injured legs.

Leg braces help kids
stand and move.

Some kids who wear

leg braces are born

with weak bones or muscles.

Other kids wear leg braces

because they were injured.

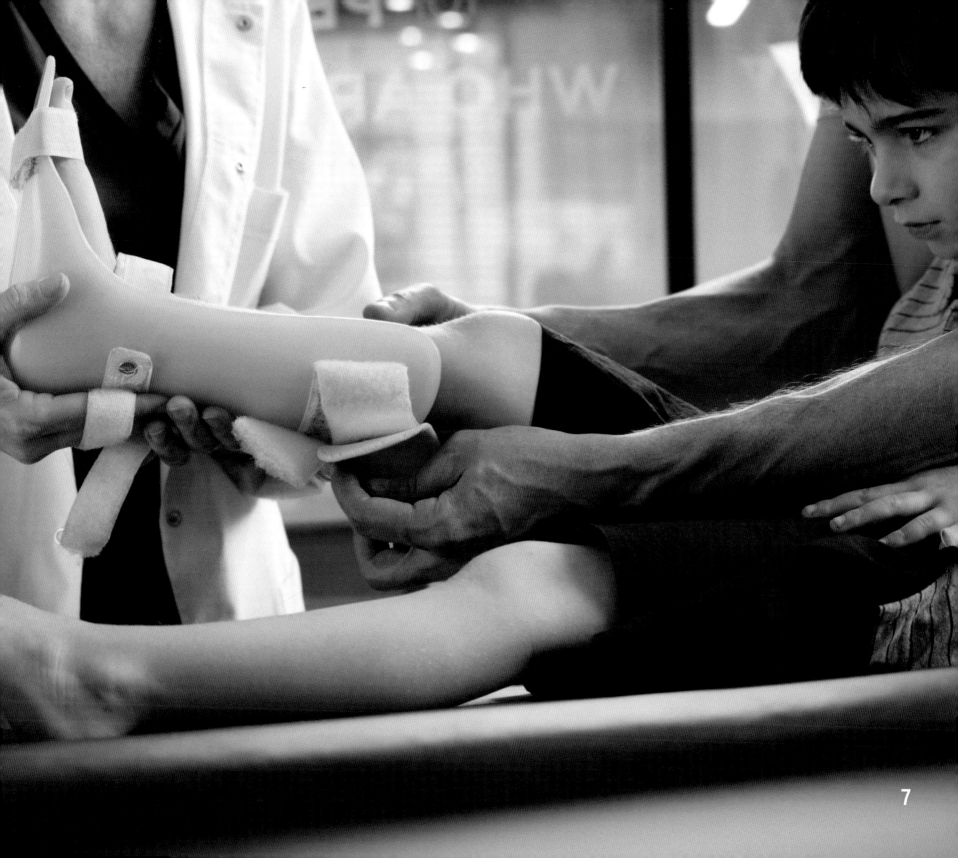

Some kids start wearing
leg braces when they are
very young.

9

Leg braces are different colours and sizes.

Leg braces cover the whole leg or only part of the leg.

Physiotherapists teach kids

to use leg braces.

They teach kids how

to exercise and move.

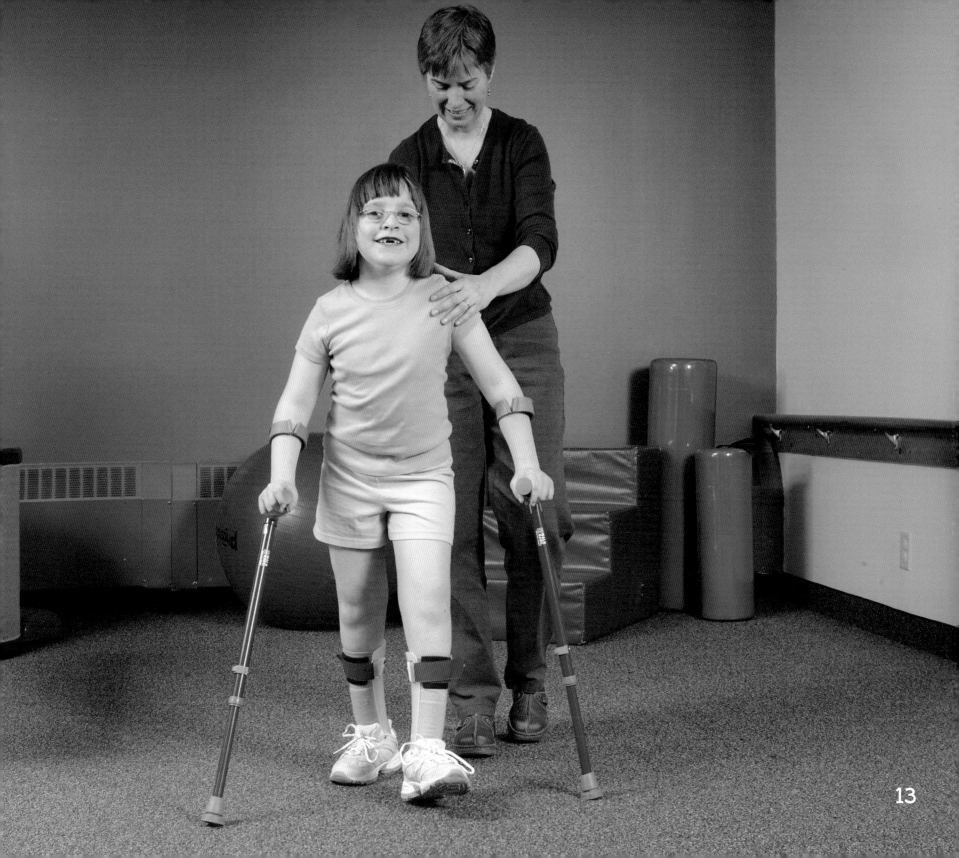

Everyday life

Some kids who wear

leg braces use walkers

or crutches.

They go for walks.

Kids who wear leg braces help

at home.

They dust or do other jobs.

Kids who wear leg braces

study and do homework.

Kids who wear leg braces like

to have fun.

They play with their friends.

Glossary

crutch long wooden or metal stick with a padded top; people with leg injuries often use crutches to help them walk

exercise physical activity that a person does to keep fit and healthy

injured damaged or hurt; some people wear leg braces because they were injured

physiotherapist person trained to give treatment to people who are hurt or have physical disabilities; massage and exercise are two kinds of treatment

support help to hold something in place; leg braces support weak joints and injured legs and feet

walker metal frame with four legs and wheels that supports people when they walk; walkers improve balance and stability

Find out more

Books

Having a Disability (Questions and Feelings About), Louise Spilsbury (Franklin Watts, 2017)

We All Have Different Abilities (Celebrating Differences), Melissa Higgins (Raintree, 2017)

Websites

Information about living with a disabled sibling: https://www.sibs.org.uk/

Find out how the StandProud charity is helping disabled children in Congo by providing them with leg braces: http://www.standproud.org.uk/11.html

Comprehension questions

1. Describe reasons why some kids wear leg braces.

2. How does wearing leg braces help some kids?

3. What does a physical therapist do to help kids who wear leg braces?

Index